MY MAPLE TREE

A tale of my maple tree
from seed to tree to seed.

This book authored by Kevin D. Finson.
All photos and illustrations by Kevin D. Finson.

Independently Published. ISBN 9798446405800

This book is dedicated to my grandchildren, that their interest in and love of nature will always be close to their hearts.

Come here and see my maple tree!
It started from a tiny seed.
It grew and grew up to the sky,
And now it reaches oh so high!

This seed just floated on the wind,
    And in my lawn was journey's end.
It nestled down into the grass,
    And waited for some time to pass.

One day, then two, then three went by,
And then a sprout peeked at the sky.
It started very tiny first,
But then it grew with quite a burst!

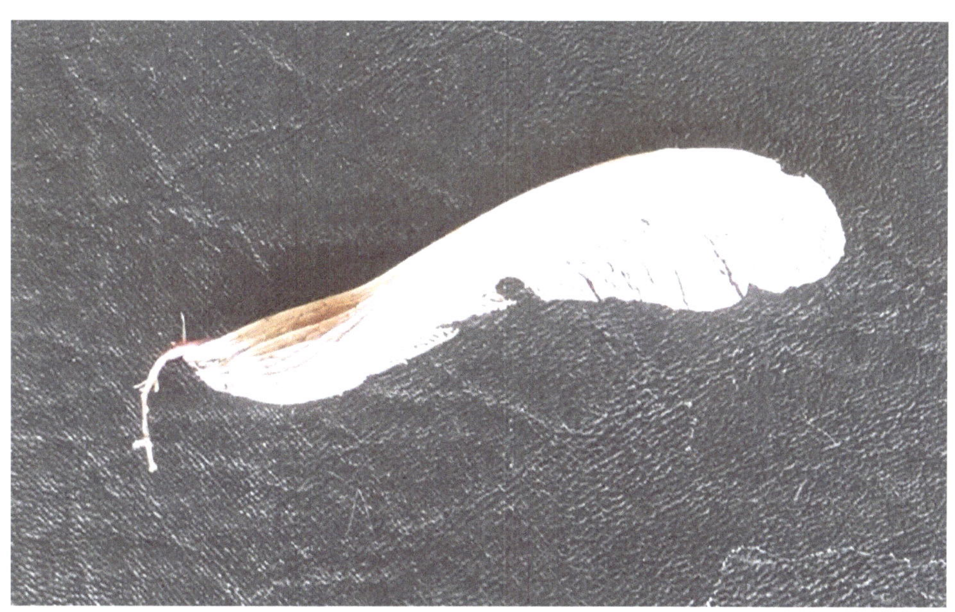

3

That seed became a baby tree.
    And then was plain for all to see:
What once was just a tiny seed
    Was now a tiny maple tree!

Its roots reached down into the ground,
Its little trunk was greenish-brown.
Its leaves spread out to catch the sun,
A brand new sapling had begun!

From its top did branches shoot,
    They soon were higher than our roof!
Its branches new were tender red,
    And leaves would spring from buds
    that led.

Each tiny bud was tightly round,
    Inside each one its leaves were bound.
But soon the buds would open up,
    Releasing leaves we like so much!

From all the buds the leaves did come,
  Shot forth in clusters, not just one.
The baby leaves now free at last
  Could open wide and grow so fast!

And with the leaves as they did sprout,
   Then longer reached the branches out.
From them more buds and leaves would show
   To catch the sun, and with it grow.

What once were tiny pinkish leaves
	Next grew and spread, and sunlight
	seized.
Their green made food the tree did need,
	Its sugars were so nice, indeed!

And up and up, that tree did soar,
    It spread its branches ever more!
And made a home for birds so neat,
    To hear them sing was such a treat!

Throughout the day its work be done,
It needed water, and the sun.
It graced us with its cooling shade,
With breezes rustling music made.

When by that tree we laid aside,
   And tried to peek up to the sky,
All that before us was revealed
   Was green and green and shading still.

To climb a little up the trunk,
    Was not as easy as we thunk.
The squirrels just seem to scamper by,
    And up they run the branches high.

Then when the summer's run is done,
  The green does fade, the reds will
  come.
The colors change first at the top
  Then downward move until it stops.

And once the change has run its course,
A brilliant beauty from its source,
The leaves are dressed in scarlet bright,
An awesome and so pretty sight!

Finally in their final glory red,
    Soon did we see the leaves were shed.
At first just one, and then some more,
    Until the tree had leaves no more.

And just before the snows did fly,
    We through the branches viewed the
    sky.
So sad to see the tree bereft,
    With not a single leaf still left.

The tree trunk's bark now seemed like
white,
    But it was just the low sun's light.
Now was the time the tree to sleep,
    To make it through the winter deep.

Midwinter snows then blankets laid,
    With frigid winds that blew each day.
Pure whiteness settled on the ground,
    And scarcely was there any sound.

20

Yet in the cold and white the tree
    Without its green or red to see,
There was a beauty to behold,
    While sleeping was the tree once bold.

And then the snows away did melt,
And subtle warmth the tree it felt.
In early spring, chilled air still hung,
But then tree growth was soon begun.

Before we knew it, tiny leaves
   Popped out from all around that tree!
With joy we knew the spring was come,
   Those tiny leaves showed winter done.

Overnight it seemed they sprouted,
    From their buds, new red was shouted.
From that first day's so wrinkly start
    Soon little leaves would look so smart!

And with the newest leaves did form
    Some baby seeds like from a horn!
Announcing some new life to come,
    Nature's work is never done.

Almost before we winked our eye,
    That tree dropped seeds into the sky.
Each sought its home upon the wind,
    To grow more trees and start again!

In case you are interested for educational purposes, this book addresses some of the current science education standards set forth in the *Next Generation Science Standards for States, by States* developed by twenty six state partners, the National Research Council, the National Science Teachers Association, and the American Association for the Advancement of Science.

NGSS Disciplinary Core standard LS1.A (Structure and function) about organisms having structures that allow for growth and reproduction;

NGSS Disciplinary Core standard LS1.B (Growth and development of organisms) about reproduction being essential to every kind of organisms and organisms have unique and diverse life cycles;

NGSS Crosscutting Relationships 3-LS4-4 (as the environment changes the plants therein also change); and

NGSS Crosscutting Literacy Reading Anchor RST.6-8-2 (provide an accurate summary of the text distinct from prior knowledge or opinions.)

About the Author

Kevin Finson is a retired professor of science education. He taught 34 years at the college level, two at the high school level, and five at the middle school level. He is an earth scientist by training, but also has taught physical, life, and other sciences (as well as teaching on instructional theory and program evaluation). He is a vocal proponent of inquiry learning and teaching. Kevin has a sense of humor and really likes puns and shaggy dog stories. When at the university, he hosted an annual holiday party featuring a shaggy dog story contest. Since his retirement, he started to write children's books for his grandchildren. During his working career, Kevin was heavily involved in service to professional science education associations and maintained a consistent publication record that included the publication of eight books, some chapters and monographs, and a host of refereed (peer-reviewed) journal articles. Most of his professional academic publication focus has been on science for students with disabilities and on students' perceptions about scientists and visual data.

This book is written for children ages 5 through 12. It is the story of how a thunderstorm forms and then passes. It is written in a rhyming narrative and includes original photographs of clouds.

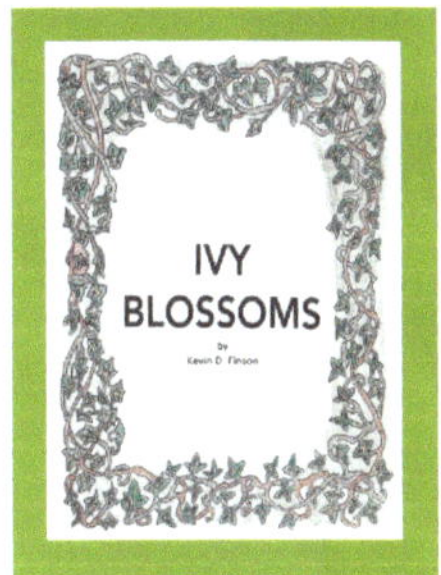

This book is written for children ages 3 through 8 and presents the color spectrum nature reveals through flower blossoms. It is written in a rhyming narrative and includes original photographs of flower blossoms.

Christmas was coming, and Annie had no idea what to get for her mother as a present. What could she possibly get her mother that would show her how much she loved her? She had to make a decision sometime in the twelve days that were left before Christmas arrived. Come and journey with Annie each of those days as she searches for that perfect present. Then, discover what that very best gift actually was!

What was Starduster's purpose and role in God's plan to fill the universe with light and warmth? Come and share in Starduster's story as the very first star created by God in His plan to pierce the cold darkness of space and bring life into it. See how Starduster gave of itself in God's plan to make billions of stars and planets, and more specifically how it led to the creation of the earth and life on it. Find out how Starduster's legacy lives on in the guiding light illuminated by the Bethlehem Star. This story was inspired by a letter Kevin wrote to his granddaughter.

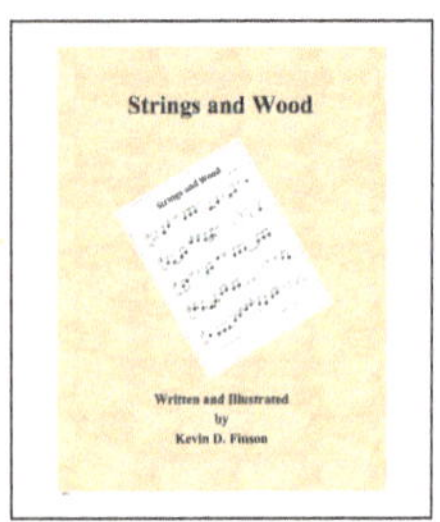

The mysterious guitar was found in an old attic. Nobody knew where it came from, how it came to be in the attic of the old house, or even how long it had been there. It wasn't until someone in the family decided to dust it off and begin playing it that its healing wonders were revealed. Not everyone wanted the healing music to be heard and tried to destroy the guitar. Yet the healing music was resurrected from the shattered remains of the guitar and would not be silenced.

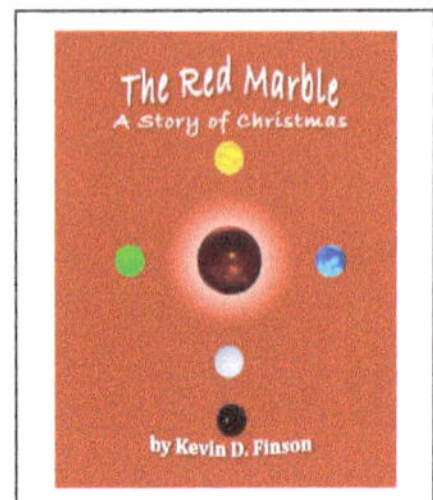

Leo's friend at school was from a very poor family, and Leo wanted to give him something very special for Christmas. While shopping during the week just before Christmas, Leo finds his way into an old toy shop where the owner shares with him the loving histories of six very special marbles. Leo knows they would be the perfect gift for his friend, but he is unable to buy them. Leo returns home saddened that his mission to get something for his friend has failed, but is surprised on Christmas morning by finding out he has succeeded beyond his dreams.

The mysterious seed came upon the winds blowing from heaven. It came to rest on the shore of a mountain lake where it sprouted and grew into a beautiful tree full of rainbow colors. A little girl discovers the tree and finds peace and solace in its beauty. But her peace is ruined by a storm that rages through the mountains. What happens to her rainbow tree? Will the little girl's peace and comfort be gone forever, or will it be restored – not only for her, but for others, too? Come read this allegorical story about the coming of Jesus, the storm that seemed to break Him, and His resurrection in the lives of people throughout the world.

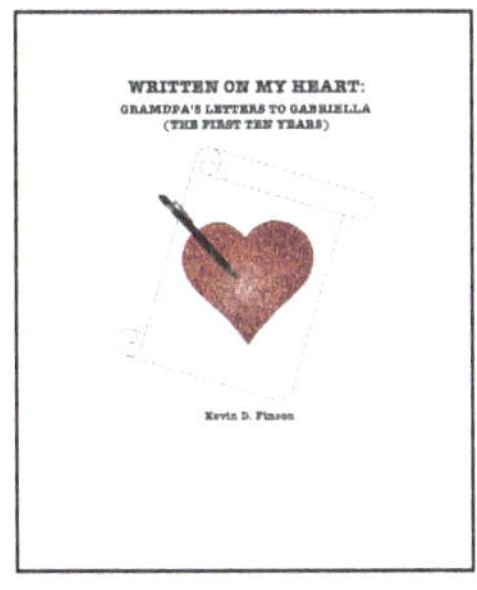  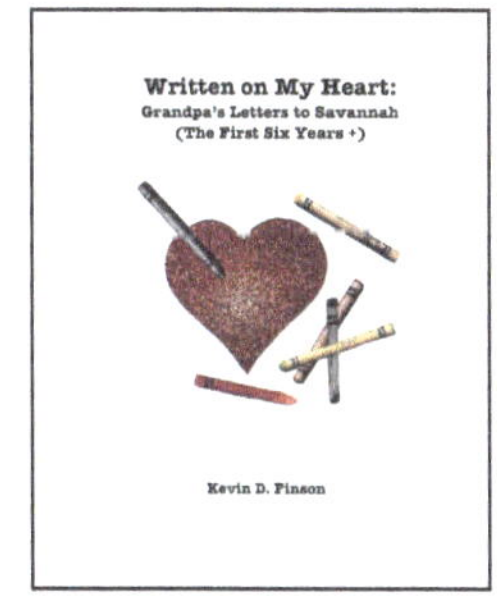

Travel along the road of life with Kevin and his granddaughters. He has undertaken the loving task of sharing with them episodic memories of his and their lives mixed with touches of science and history. From the day his grandchildren were born Kevin decided to write letters to Gabriella, Ivy, and Savannah each month, most of them on the day of the month on which each was born. This book is a compilation of the first ten years' worth of letters Kevin wrote to Gabriella, the first eight years to Ivy, and the first six to Savannah. It is through such letters that one can come closer to family and become more understanding of one's roots. These letters are more than just a diary since Kevin wrote them to his grandchildren rather than to himself. The purpose of each letter is to provide short stories in the context of real life and how it relates to growth and development in one's faith in God. The central message is to seek ways to have a strong faith and unwavering trust in God as she navigates the roads of life that lie before her.